Marilyn Monroe

Marilyn Monroe

Marie Clayton

PULTENEY
PRESS

Published by International Book Marketing Ltd
First published in 2008

Pulteney Press
1 Riverside Court
St Johns Road
Bath, BA2 6PD, UK

© Atlantic Publishing
For details of picture copyrights see page 96

Opposite: Norma Jeane Baker, aged about fourteen, before she became the legend that was Marilyn Monroe. The daughter of film cutter Gladys Baker, the young Norma Jeane never knew who her father was and spent much of a rather unsettled childhood in a succession of orphanages and foster homes. She married James Dougherty, the son of a neighbor, when she was only just sixteen – perhaps mainly because this promised to bring some stability into her life. Less than two years after their marriage the demands of wartime meant that James was posted abroad on active service for an extended period.

Right: An early professional portrait. Army photographer David Conover had discovered Norma Jeane working at a munitions factory and since she looked so good on camera he recommended she try a career as a model. She soon signed up with the Blue Book Agency, who suggested she lighten her red-brown hair and sent her to classes in make-up and grooming. Marilyn soon became a successful model and she and her husband separated, although they did not actually divorce until 1946.

Left: In 1946 a screen test with Twentieth Century Fox led to a six-month contract and a series of small parts in B movies. At the same time the studio decided that Norma Jeane should change her name, so she selected Monroe, her grandmother's surname. The name Marilyn was chosen by the studio, after stage actress Marilyn Miller. Fox renewed Marilyn's contract at the end of the first six months, but at the end of the year they dropped her. However, in the meantime she had met Joe Schenck, co-founder of Fox, at a Hollywood party and he persuaded Columbia Studios to hire her instead.

Opposite: At Columbia Marilyn met drama coach Natasha Lytess, who became her personal teacher. The aspiring actress was also given her first proper part in a film, as Peggy Martin in *Ladies of the Chorus*. She got good reviews, but at the end of the first six months Columbia also chose not to exercise its option to renew her contract.

Left: Marilyn smiles for the camera. She told reporters later that when her first film was released she wished that the name on the marquee could have been Norma Jeane rather than Marilyn, so that everyone who had put her down in the past could see it.

Opposite: An early publicity picture of Marilyn taken to promote her film *Ladies of the Chorus*, in which she played singer Peggy Martin.

Above and opposite: Marilyn's cameo role in *Love Happy* was as a gorgeous blonde client of private detective Sam Grunion, played by Groucho Marx. Although the part was a small one, it certainly got her noticed by studio executives and with influential agent Johnny Hyde now working tirelessly on her behalf it seemed as if Marilyn's career would soon take off.

Above and opposite: Marilyn at a WWSC microphone during a *Photoplay Magazine* contest event, in
Williamsburg, New York in 1949. She was in New York City to promote *Love Happy*, and had traveled
to Williamsburg to present the contest winner with the key to a new house.

Above: Marilyn pictured with James Brown and Mickey Rooney in *The Fireball*, which was released in 1950. Marilyn had a small role in the movie.

Opposite: A rare early casual shot of Marilyn, taken in 1950 during a photo session in Johnny Hyde's backyard in Beverly Hills. Johnny and Marilyn had met at a New Year's Eve party and afterwards he had invited her out. Before long he had left his wife to devote himself to Marilyn.

Right: Due to the efforts of Johnny Hyde Marilyn appeared in several films in 1950, including *Ticket to Tomahawk* and *Right Cross*. She was also offered a small but very good part in *The Asphalt Jungle*, directed by John Huston. She only had three scenes in the movie, but managed to make quite an impact.

Opposite: Marilyn in *Home Town Story*, a film that was not released commercially. Produced by General Motors to promote American industry, the movie features Marilyn as a secretary to a politician who is convinced that big business is behind his election loss.

Opposite and right: Marilyn poses for some obligatory cheesecake shots as required by the studio. All contract players were expected to attend regular photographic sessions and Hollywood events. Marilyn was always happy to oblige, since she knew her career could depend on someone in a position of importance noticing her. All the photographers who worked with Marilyn commented on how professional and hardworking she was at photoshoots. By now her hair was truly blonde – she was to keep it this color for the rest of her life, although the exact shade varied.

Opposite: Classes in dance, singing
and drama were part of a contract
player's life. Marilyn had fallen in
love with her voice coach –
Columbia's handsome, thirty-two-
year-old director of music, Fred
Karger – but he did not return her
regard.

Right: Agent Johnny Hyde did love
Marilyn – he constantly urged her
to marry him. He paid for minor
cosmetic surgery, bought her a
wardrobe full of beautiful clothes
and introduced her to the top
Hollywood society. Marilyn cared
deeply for Johnny but would not
consent to be his wife, partly
because she was not in love with
him and partly because she feared
that as the wife of an influential
agent she would not be taken
seriously. It was a decision that
rebounded on her – when Johnny
died of a heart attack in December
1950 his family threw her out of
the house and took back
everything he had given her.

Left: Between 1946 and 1951 Marilyn was just one of many aspiring starlets in the studio system. All of them were beautiful and talented – but most of them would never make that final step to full superstardom. What set Marilyn apart was her determination to be someone and an ability to turn on a magnetic personality for the camera at will, although by all accounts she was often very shy and quiet in person.

Right: Another talent that became apparent in later years was Marilyn's sense of humor and natural comedy timing. Some of her best movies are comedies, although she always aspired to be a serious actress.

Opposite: Before Johnny Hyde died he had managed to get Marilyn a good part in the film *All About Eve*, which was one of the most successful movies of 1950. As a result, Marilyn caught the eye of studio head Darryl Zanuck and was finally offered the coveted long-term contract. Listening carefully to directions from Gregory Ratoff in this picture are (clockwise from left to right) actors Anne Baxter, Gary Merrill, Celeste Holm, George Sanders and Marilyn. *All About Eve* was directed by respected professional Joseph L. Mankiewicz.

Right: By this time, Marilyn had several good parts under her belt, but it would be another year before her career really took off.

Opposite: Marilyn had been taught how to apply make-up at an early age and she was an expert at making the best of her natural looks. In later years she was often late, both for appointments and on set, as she would sit in front of her mirror for hours getting ready. This was not vanity – she just needed everything to be perfect before she could appear.

Right: By the end of 1950 Marilyn's contract was up for renewal again and without Johnny Hyde behind her the outcome was looking doubtful – even though she had acquitted herself well in the roles she had been given. As usual Marilyn refused to give up and managed to get her contract renewed by attending a dinner for exhibitors in a skin-tight cocktail dress that showed off her curves to their very best advantage.

In 1951 Marilyn was loaned to RKO to appear in *Clash By Night*, directed by the renowned Fritz Lang. It was the first major dramatic role she had been offered, and even though it was not a large part she threw herself into it and received excellent reviews. Twentieth Century Fox finally realized that they had a potential star on their hands and they began to look for the right movie in which she could take a leading role.

Just as it seemed success was assured, disaster struck again. When Marilyn had been a struggling young actress she had posed nude for a photographer and in 1952 the picture of an unknown blonde stretched out on red velvet was used for a calendar. This was soon displayed in gas stations across the country – and it wasn't long before people began to recognize Fox's rising star. The studio wanted to deny that it was Marilyn, but she faced the press and explained that she had needed money to eat and pay her rent, and that had been the only honest way she could earn it. She also said the photographer's wife had been present as a chaperon. The public were sympathetic and instead of ruining her career the calendar was reprinted many times.

Above and opposite: Marilyn at the Star of Tomorrow Awards on January 26, 1952 in Los Angeles, California. She had won a trophy as one of the promising starlets who were predicted to have a great future. A few months after this event Marilyn hit the headlines again when it was discovered that she wasn't an orphan, as the studio had told everyone. The press had found her mother, who had been living in a series of state mental institutions, but Marilyn released a short statement saying that she had only just discovered the truth herself. Since it soon became apparent that she had been supporting her mother financially for the last year, again the public forgave her and her career continued to thrive.

Left and opposite: Marilyn's first major role was in *Niagara* as Rose Loomis, a sultry seductress who plans with her lover to murder her husband. The plan goes terribly wrong and Rose and her lover are the ones who are killed. The movie features a famous sequence in which Marilyn walks away from the camera, her hips swaying provocatively. It caused a sensation – and Marilyn's future was assured.

Marilyn's private life was also attracting attention. Baseball superstar Joe DiMaggio had seen her picture and asked who she was. One of his teammates happened to know Marilyn, and an introduction was soon arranged. Dinner followed and soon Joe was calling Marilyn nightly and their romance was documented in all the newspapers. Marilyn not only loved Joe himself but also the feeling of warmth and security that his close family gave her – something that she had never had before.

Opposite: Marilyn and Jane Russell in one of her most famous movies, *Gentlemen Prefer Blondes*. Fox had bought the rights to the story for established star Betty Grable, but director Howard Hawks convinced them that Marilyn would be better in the role. She threw herself into the part with her usual enthusiasm, but it was also on this movie that her chronic lateness began to become an issue. She would lock herself in her dressing room for hours after she was supposed to be on set, a habit which many saw as evidence of unprofessionalism or simply rudeness.

Right: Marilyn and Jane Russell about to leave their handprints in the pavement outside the famous Grauman's Chinese Theater. It was Jane who realized that Marilyn was not being rude by failing to arrive on set – she couldn't appear until she had worked herself up to the point where she felt everything was perfect and she could perform. It was this intensity that made Marilyn unique on camera.

Right and opposite: Glamor shots of Marilyn. Even as early as this in her career she was being thought of as a dumb blonde, and her first screen roles were all based around this perception. She soon created a beautiful, funny, innocent – but sexy – persona that the public adored. However, Marilyn always wanted a more serious image and spent much of her later career trying to achieve this. Many respected directors came to believe that she did have amazing talent and that she would mature into an astonishing dramatic actress.

Left: Immediately after filming finished on *Gentlemen Prefer Blondes* Marilyn began work on her next movie, *How to Marry a Millionaire*. The cast also included Betty Grable and Lauren Bacall and the film was directed by Jean Negulesco and produced by Twentieth Century Fox. The storyline was designed to build on the success of Marilyn's previous film – but having had no break between them she was exhausted and emotionally drained. Her character was very short-sighted, but refused to wear glasses – which gave rise to many of the jokes in the script and confirmed how good she was at comedy.

Opposite: Lauren Bacall and Humphrey Bogart with Marilyn at the premiere of How to Marry a Millionaire in July 1953. Marilyn was still dating Joe DiMaggio regularly, but he preferred to keep out of the limelight as far as she was concerned and very rarely appeared at showbusiness events with her.

Right: A rare candid shot of Marilyn on set. After she died, Billy Wilder – respected director of The Seven Year Itch and Some Like It Hot – said of her: "She was an absolute genius as a comedic actress, with an extraordinary sense for comedic dialogue. It was a God-given gift. Believe me, in the last fifteen years there were ten projects that came to me, and I'd start working on them and I'd think, 'It's not going to work, it needs Marilyn Monroe.' Nobody else is in that orbit; everyone else is earthbound by comparison."

Left: In many photographs of Marilyn taken to promote her career or her current movie, she is not wearing her own clothes. The studio would often lend outfits to up-and-coming actors so they could appear in public looking like film stars.

Opposite: The expensive jewelry that Marilyn sports in many publicity shots and in pictures taken at official events was also not usually her own. She had little interest in jewelry and owned very few pieces herself, instead borrowing items from the studio wardrobe department or later from jewelers.

Opposite and right: Marilyn and her co-star, Robert Mitchum, in *River of No Return*. Directed by Otto Preminger and filmed in Canada in 1953, the picture was beset with problems. Marilyn had come straight from her previous movie again, with little rest in between, and her agent was becoming concerned about the effect of continuous work – both on her health and because of a danger of overexposure in her career. On top of this Marilyn fell and hurt her leg on some rocks on location, which delayed filming by several days, and the schedule finally overran by some weeks When the studio decided that she was to start work on *The Girl in Pink Tights* straight after filming on *River of No Return* finished, both Marilyn and her agent decided it was time to take a stand. Marilyn was also annoyed that no one seemed to think it was necessary that she should see a full copy of the script – and from the synopsis it was evident that she was to play yet another dumb blonde.

Opposite: Even for this casual shot, lying on the grass, Marilyn was the consummate professional. Joe DiMaggio had come to visit her on the set of *River of No Return*, since they hoped to spend time together away from Hollywood to come to a decision about their future. Joe wanted them to marry – but he also wanted Marilyn to give up her career and become a full-time wife. Another bone of contention was Marilyn's need for constant adulation – Joe was very jealous and could not cope with her habit of dressing provocatively and flirting with other men, even though she had no intention of being unfaithful.

Above: Marilyn working with Baron Adolf de Meyer in Palm Springs. Baron was a leading dance, film and celebrity photographer, who often worked for *Vogue* and *Vanity Fair*.

Above: After *River of No Return* was completed, Marilyn became involved in a row with the studio when she refused to start work on *The Girl in Pink Tights*. Joe took part in negotiations in a bid to protect her interests and perhaps Marilyn saw this as evidence that he was happy for her to continue working, as soon afterwards she finally agreed to marry him.

Opposite: Baron took some wonderful photographs of a casual and relaxed-looking Marilyn

Opposite: In January 1954 Marilyn and Joe DiMaggio were finally married, in San Francisco. Marilyn only told the studio of the wedding on the day, but the publicity machine immediately swung into action and pictures of the happy couple soon appeared in all the newspapers.

Right: Marilyn, looking radiant, is escorted by Joe soon after their marriage. Unfortunately the happiness was not to last.

Above: After the honeymoon, the studio expected Marilyn to report for work on *The Girl in Pink Tights*, as ordered. However, Marilyn still refused to make the movie, partly because she didn't like what she had seen of the script, and partly because her agent was now negotiating for more money, as well as script and director approval. The studio reacted to her continued absence by putting her on suspension, so Marilyn flew to Japan with Joe as an extension of their honeymoon. While she was in the area she took a few days to go to Korea to entertain US troops stationed there. During her days as a starlet she had been a pin-up for the army, and felt she owed them for the boost to her career.

Opposite: Marilyn visiting Marlon Brando in 1954 on the set of *Desiree*, in which he was playing Napoleon. Meanwhile the studio had backed down on *The Girl in Pink Tights*, offering Marilyn a hastily created part in *There's No Business Like Show Business* instead, along with a promise of the lead in *The Seven Year Itch*. However, they would not give her the creative control she wanted, so Marilyn soon began working on other plans.

Opposite: Agent Charles Feldman had succeeded in getting Marilyn a raise in salary and in future she would be consulted about the choice of coach and choreographer on her films. She reported for work on *There's No Business Like Show Business* but she was still recovering from the pneumonia caught entertaining troops in Korea. Despite her best efforts the movie did not do well, and Marilyn was confirmed in her view that the studio was not choosing the best projects for her talents.

Above: Marilyn and Dan Dailey on the set of *There's No Business Like Show Business*. Marilyn's part had been added to the film at the last minute, and she was given some musical numbers originally written for Ethel Merman, a professional singer with a powerful voice. Marilyn worked hard with her voice and dance coaches, so her performance would not be overshadowed by the more experienced performers in the cast.

Opposite: Much of the filming of *The Seven Year Itch* was done on location in New York. Marilyn played the perfect dumb blonde – her character does not even have a name. The famous scene in which Marilyn stands over a subway grating allowing her white skirt to blow up indirectly led to the ending of her marriage to Joe, who had been persuaded to come and watch the sequence being filmed. The sight of his wife displaying her underwear to thousands of cheering New Yorkers was just too much for his jealous nature to take, and the following day he left for California. By October they had filed for divorce.

Above: Marilyn and Tom Ewell in a scene from *The Seven Year Itch*. He plays Richard, who remains in New York to work during a heat wave, after his wife and young son have retreated to the cool of the country. Marilyn's character rents the apartment upstairs and her innocent sexuality sparks a host of fantasies in her hapless neighbor. In the event Richard decides to join his wife and son, leaving Marilyn to enjoy the air conditioning in the family apartment.

Above and opposite: Marilyn and Donald O'Connor at the premiere of *There's No Business Like Show Business*. Although on the surface Marilyn was complying with studio demands, privately she was talking to photographer Milton Greene about forming her own production company, so she could choose the roles she played. At the end of December 1954 Marilyn Monroe Productions was formed; the official announcement was made public at a Press conference on January 7, 1955.

Left and opposite: Marilyn in a series of casual photographs taken at her home in California. However, she spent most of 1955 in New York, developing her acting skills at the Actors' Studio with Lee Strasberg. As soon as she had announced the formation of her own company Fox began the fight to keep its biggest star, pointing out that she was under an exclusive contract to them for the next four years. Luckily, lawyers for Marilyn Monroe Productions found that Fox had breached the contract on several occasions and so they were able to declare it null and void.

Left: At the end of 1955 Marilyn signed a new contract with Fox. The new deal gave her a much more lucrative financial package as well as approval of script, director and cinematographer. She not only received a percentage of the film's profits, but also had unprecedented creative control of her projects.

Opposite: Marilyn's new deal also allowed her to work on one independent project a year, and she was quick to take advantage of this. Here she is seen in 1956 with Laurence Olivier at a press conference in New York, at which they announced their forthcoming collaboration to film *The Prince and the Showgirl*. Marilyn was particularly keen to appear with Olivier, since she felt that his reputation as a serious classical actor would change people's view of her – she was desperate to be seen as a real actress. Conversely Olivier's glittering career had stalled, so he hoped appearing with Marilyn would revitalize it. The project also gave him the opportunity to co-produce and direct.

Left: Marilyn at a press conference in Los Angeles in 1956. She returned to Hollywood a much more confident and mature person – she had taken on the studio system and won. She fully expected to be given credit for her bravery and to be taken much more seriously, but ironically many saw her actions as turning her back on Hollywood, which had put her where she was.

Opposite: Before she left for England to work with Olivier, Marilyn was to star in *Bus Stop*, her first film since the new contract had been agreed. Seen here in a candid shot taken on the set, she adjusts her make-up using a handheld mirror.

Opposite: Marilyn with Don Murray, her co-star on *Bus Stop*. Studio bosses were concerned that she would make impossible demands to test her new power, but Marilyn was determined to prove she was not just a dumb blonde. Her first action was to throw out all the elaborate costumes designed for her and to select a series of tattered secondhand outfits from the studio wardrobe instead – she felt the worn clothes were more appropriate for her character of a down-at-heel bar-room girl. Director Joshua Logan was won over immediately, and his opinion was confirmed after Lee Strasberg told him of Marilyn's outstanding performances at the Actors' Studio.

Right: Costumes like this showed off Marilyn's hourglass figure to best advantage. During *Bus Stop* she had to be hospitalized for several days after coming down with a severe case of bronchitis – she often suffered from bronchial problems.

Opposite and left: Marilyn had first met playwright Arthur Miller in 1950, but they got to know each other in New York in 1955. Miller was married with two children, but his marriage was already in trouble and he and Marilyn quickly found they were attracted to each other. Despite the apparent odds against their relationship developing, while Marilyn was filming *Bus Stop* Miller went to Nevada to get a divorce. Back in New York in June 1956 they married secretly – but the press soon got wind of the nuptials. Marilyn was used to all the attention, but it was all a big shock to Miller. He hoped that things would quieten down after the wedding – little did he realize that life with Marilyn would always be conducted in the spotlight.

Opposite: Marilyn with Arthur Miller and Milton Greene. Miller planned to accompany Marilyn to England when she went to film *The Prince and the Showgirl*, but this was at the height of the witch-hunts against Communism and he had previously flirted with the Communist Party. Despite this, he was finally given his passport and the two of them flew to England in July 1956.

Right: Miller and Marilyn at a press call to welcome the American star to England. The trip was the first time that the new couple had spent an extended amount of time together and it put a big strain on their relationship. Miller had no idea until then how insecure Marilyn could be when she was working and he quickly realized just how much support he would be called upon to offer. He not only found this emotionally draining; he also discovered that he could not work effectively on his writing at the same time.

Opposite: A Georgian house on the edge of Windsor Great Park had been rented for Marilyn to occupy during filming. She appeared to be a changed woman, standing proudly next to her intellectual husband, about to begin work on the first film being made by her own new production company.

Right: Olivier and his wife Vivien Leigh had both come to welcome the Millers to England. In America Olivier had announced that he planned to "fall shatteringly in love" with Marilyn – but now she was married to Miller and his own wife had recently announced that she was pregnant. Under the circumstances he was much more circumspect and distant with Marilyn – but unfortunately she took his attitude personally.

Left and opposite: While in London Marilyn and Miller attended the London première of his new play, *A View from the Bridge*. Large crowds flocked to see the production – chiefly because of the publicity generated by Marilyn's presence. She was working very hard to earn Miller's approval, which she felt she had lost when she had miscarried their first child after only a few weeks.

Opposite and right: Marilyn on set during filming of *The Prince and the Showgirl* – which was known by its original title of *The Sleeping Prince* during production. The production process was not really a happy time for many of those involved, however. Olivier was angered by Marilyn's chronic lateness, while Marilyn felt that he constantly undermined her on set. Despite this, Marilyn turned out her usual luminous performance and the movie turned out to be a great success. Olivier soon forgot the problems of actually working with Marilyn, and later said of her: "She is a brilliant comedienne, which to me means she also is an extremely skilled actress."

Opposite: Marilyn with photographer Milton Greene. He had first taken pictures of her in 1953, and she felt he had illustrated aspects of her character that others had not seen. He was keen to break into movie production, and Marilyn's disillusion with the studio had provided the ideal opportunity. At first things went very well, but Miller came to distrust Greene's abilities and soon convinced Marilyn that Greene was not working in her best interests. Miller eventually convinced Marilyn to fire him – which she agreed to do in an attempt to save her failing marriage. Later she told Greene's wife Amy that she regretted this decision, as she realized just how much he had achieved for her.

Left: Marilyn at the theater with Arthur Miller. If she wanted to be private she would cover her hair, keep in the background and no one would notice her. Sometimes she couldn't resist turning into Marilyn though – and people who saw the transformation commented that it was if she had flicked an internal switch, suddenly turning on a powerful attraction that brought people flocking around her.

Opposite: At the April in Paris Ball of 1957 Marilyn chats to Ambassador Winthrop Aldrich, ex-envoy to Britain, as her husband Arthur Miller looks on. While Marilyn was away in England the movie *Bus Stop* had been released. She was deeply disappointed that her long dramatic monologue had been severely cut, but the film received glowing reviews and almost everyone decided that Marilyn had proved she really could act.

Right: Marilyn's next project was the 1958 film *Some Like It Hot*, directed by Billy Wilder.

Left: *Some Like It Hot* co-starred Tony Curtis and Jack Lemmon. Marilyn had initially wanted to turn the project down, feeling that her character, Sugar Kane, was truly a dumb blonde if she did not realize that her two fellow band members were really men dressed as women. However, Miller pointed out that the script was outstanding so she agreed to do the film. Wilder admired Marilyn's sense of comedy but found working with her so stressful that he was driven to the edge of a nervous breakdown. The final film was a triumph – but Marilyn lost another baby toward the end of the production. It was her last attempt to become a mother.

Opposite: Marilyn and Tony Curtis on set during filming.

Left: Marilyn at a party at the end of shooting of *Some Like It Hot*. When it was released the film outgrossed all the other movies released in the same six-month period at the start of 1959, and was the most successful comedy at the box office for many years.

Opposite: British singing star Frankie Vaughan with Marilyn in a scene from *Let's Make Love*. The film was originally to star Gregory Peck as the millionaire who falls for Marilyn's character, but an actors' strike caused such a delay in filming that he had to move on to another project. He was replaced with French song-and-dance man Yves Montand.

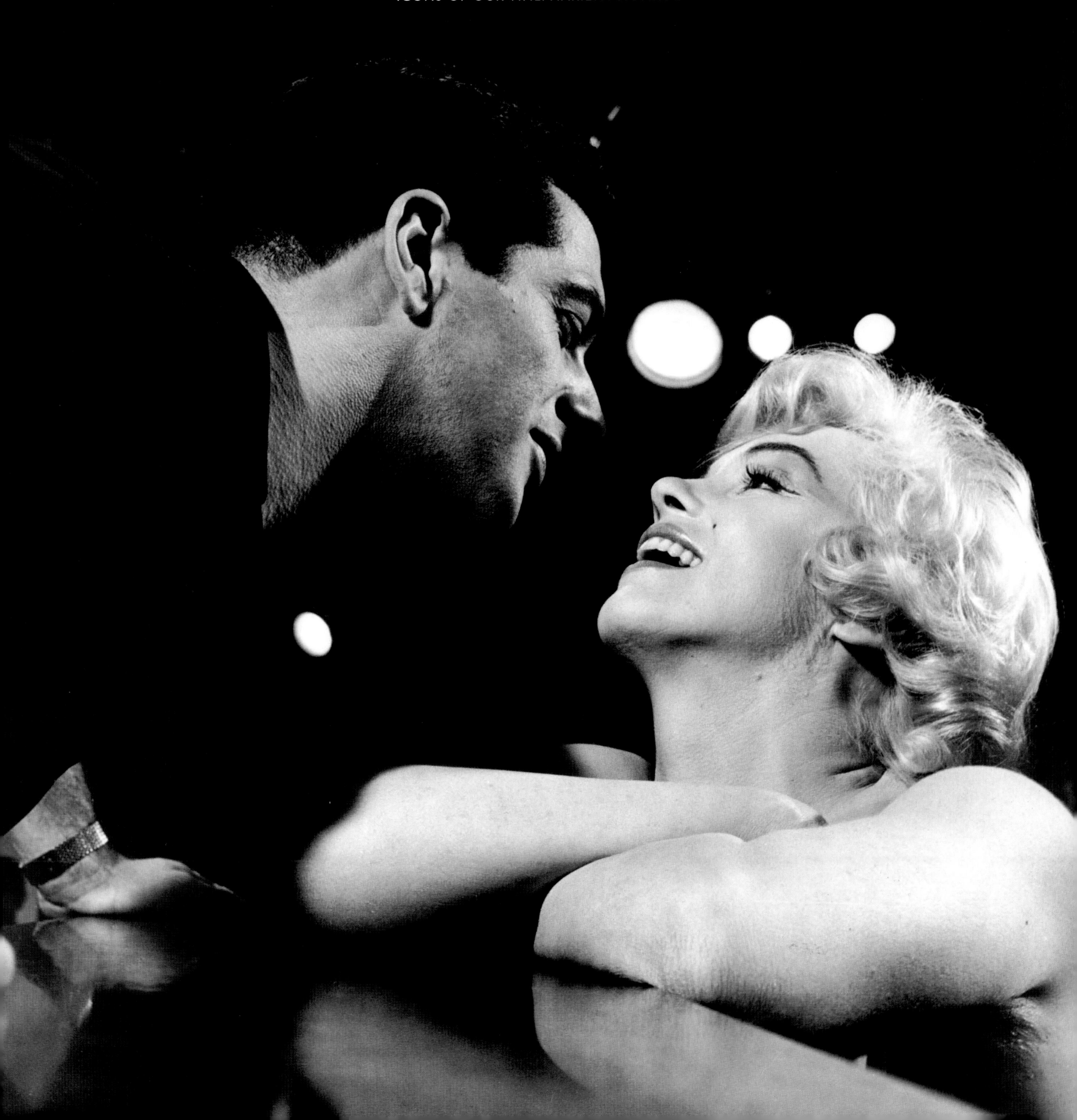

Above: Marilyn with French sex symbol Yves Montand, her co-star in *Let's Make Love*. In 1959 she had taken on the studio again and won – she had been cast in *Time and Tide*, directed by Elia Kazan, but because of delays the film did not start shooting within the terms of Marilyn's new contract. She was able to demand full payment for the film, and at the same time refuse to appear in it – and to be released from one of the movies she owed the studio. Fox was furious – but their lawyers agreed that she was completely within her rights. To recoup their losses they hurriedly cast Marilyn in *Let's Make Love*. During filming she had a brief but passionate affair with her co-star – even though both of them were married.

Opposite: Miller was completing a screenplay written specifically for Marilyn – *The Misfits*. Marilyn hoped that her husband would create a role for her that would truly showcase her talents, but he had merely written the character, Roslyn, as an idealized version of what he had once believed Marilyn to be, and the part had no depth or emotional range. She was bitterly disappointed that he had not only failed to understand her deeper moods, but had also revealed her vulnerable side for the world to see.

Right: Marilyn on the set of *The Misfits*. Filming was even more fraught than usual on a Monroe project, as Marilyn had come straight off *Let's Make Love*, with no time to build up her emotional reserves. On top of this, tensions between husband and wife spilled over onto the set. A few days after filming finished they announced their separation, and they soon divorced.

Above: Part of the filming of *The Misfits* was done in the Nevada desert, so the cast and crew were working for long days under the hot sun. Marilyn tried to keep under shade as much as possible, to protect her fair complexion. During filming she suffered from poor health and was hospitalized for a short time, suffering from exhaustion, but despite this her performance is superb.

Opposite: Eli Wallach with Marilyn in *The Misfits*. Her co-stars also included Clark Gable and Montgomery Clift. Soon after filming finished Clark Gable died of a heart attack, so this was to be

Left: Rock Hudson presents Marilyn with an award from the foreign press in March 1962. Marilyn's very fragile health had led to her being hospitalized several times during 1961, but she appeared to be back on top. She and Joe DiMaggio were seeing each other again – although only as good friends – and everything appeared to be going well. Unfortunately, when news came that Arthur Miller was to marry again, it brought back all Marilyn's old insecurities. In May 1962, during the troubled production of her last film, *Something's Got To Give*, she went absent without leave to make an appearance singing "Happy Birthday" to President Kennedy at Madison Square Garden. It was to be one of her last public appearances – on August 5, 1962, she was found dead in her Hollywood home. One of the screen's greatest stars was no more.

FILMOGRAPHY